The Constitution
by Walter A. Hazen

TABLE OF CONTENTS

McDonald Publishing Co.
12621 Western Avenue
Garden Grove, CA 92841
www.teachercreated.com

R556 • ©1996 McDonald Publishing Co.
Reprinted, 2020
ISBN: 978-1-55708-534-4
Printed in U.S.A.

Answer Key

Page 1

Answers should resemble the following:
1. to form a better kind of government for the United States
2. to treat all people equally and fairly
3. to keep the nation peaceful
4. to have armed forces for protection
5. to do what is good for all people
6. to keep everyone free

Page 2

1. F	2. T
3. T	4. T
5. F	6. T
7. F	8. T
9. T	10. T
11. F	

Page 3

1. James Madison
2. five
3. a stronger national government was needed
4. Rhode Island
5. George Washington
6. Answers will vary.

Page 4

1. James	2. Father
3. small	4. Convention
5. checks	6. American
7. draft	8. pounds
9. rights	10. president
11. Congress	12. Virginia

Page 5

1. The Virginia Plan would give too much power to states with large populations.
2. Under the New Jersey Plan, states with large populations might resent states with smaller populations having equal representation.
3. This two-house legislature allowed for fair representation for all states.
4. Answers will vary.
5. Answers will vary.

Page 6

1. 76	2. 53
3. 355	4. 10
5. Maryland	6. Pennsylvania

7. New York   8. Maryland
9. Massachusetts, New York
10. 195

Page 7

1. 25	2. 7
3. 2	4. 30
5. 9	6. 6
7. state legislatures	8. Answers will vary.
9. Answers will vary.	10. Answers will vary.

Page 8

1. expressed	2. reserved
3. implied	4. implied
5. reserved	6. expressed
7. Answers will vary.	8. Answers will vary.
9. Answers will vary.	

Page 9

1. yes	2. no
3. yes	4. yes
5. yes	6. no
7. yes	8. yes
9. no	10. no
11. no	12. yes
13. no	14. Answers will vary.

Page 10

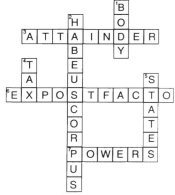

Students' answers to the short essay question will vary.

Page 11

1. He is not a natural-born citizen.
2. She is not old enough.
3. He has not lived in the U.S. for 14 years.
4. Answers will vary. A possible answer is that it is important for the president and the vice president to be able to work well together. A president from one party forced to work with a vice president from another party may not be an effective leader.

Page 12
1. make treaties; appoint ambassadors
2. serves as commander in chief of the armed forces
3. call Congress into special law-making sessions; sign and veto bills
4. grant pardons and reprieves; make appointments to the federal courts
5. make appointments to the executive branch; carry out the laws of the U.S.
6. Answers will vary.

Page 13
1. c
2. b
3. a
4. b
5. Answers will vary. Students may note that having federal judges appointed removes them from the political arena.
6. Answers will vary. Students may note that if federal judges were elected, they might give in to political pressures in order to ensure their reelection.

Page 14
1. F
2. F
3. T
4. T
5. F
6. T
7. T
8. T
9. F
10. F

Page 15
1. Yes. States must accept the records of other states.
2. Criminals could take refuge in other states and countries.
3. Possible answer: A kind of government in which people elect representatives to make laws for them.
4. In accordance with the thirteenth amendment, slavery is no longer permitted in the U.S.

Page 16
1. 38
2. 67
3. 33
4. 203
5. Possible answers: to discourage frequent changes to the Constitution, to be sure that many agree on a change before it is made, to ensure that all changes were thoroughly thought out.
6. Answers will vary.

Page 17
1. No. The Constitution requires that voters be at least eighteen years old. The state's law would be ruled unconstitutional.
2. Answers will vary, but imagined laws should be in obvious violation of the Constitution.
3. the provision about religious tests with regard to government positions. Allowing such tests would allow religion to play a part in government policy.

Page 18
1. yes
2. no
3. no
4. yes
5. no
6. no
7. yes
8. yes
9. no
10. no

Page 19
1. Possible arguments: For—it might reduce crime, make streets safer, etc. Against—it takes away one's right to bear arms, etc.
2. Answers will vary.
3. Police may obtain a search warrant if they have reason to believe a criminal is in a house, a crime has taken place in a house, stolen goods are in a house, etc.

Page 20
1. b
2. f
3. d
4. a
5. g
6. c
7. h
8. i
9. e
10. Answers will vary.

Page 21
1. Possible answers: require vaccinations for students, issue licenses to professionals, set speed limits, set health rules for restaurants, issue licenses for hunting and fishing, etc.
2. power to tax, power to pass laws, power to punish criminals
3. a. S
   b. F
   c. S
   d. S
   e. F

Page 22

1. 8
2. 2
3. 270
4. 13
5. Wyoming, .6
6. 21

Page 23

1. Poor people would find it difficult to pay a high poll tax. If a person didn't pay the tax, he couldn't vote. A literacy test could keep people without a strong education from voting.
2. They came about as a result of the Civil War.
3. Answers will vary.
4. Answers will vary.

Page 24

1. $6,400
2. $5,200
3. $4,400
4. $3,200
5. $1,200
6. $5,600
7. $4,000
8. $3,600
9. $1,600
10. $2,400
11. Answers will vary.
12. Answers will vary.

Page 25

1. The original goal was to stop the problems people believed alcohol and saloons caused.
2. Prohibition caused serious crime problems.
3. Answers will vary.

Page 26

1. 4
2. 1
3. 2
4. 6
5. 3
6. 5
7. Answers will vary.

Page 27

1. F
2. T
3. T
4. F
5. F
6. F
7. F
8. T
9. F
10. T

Page 28

Answers should resemble the following:
1. To ensure an organized government; to protect the individual rights of citizens.
2. A constitution generally states two things: the kind of government a nation will have and how it is to be chosen, and the individual rights of citizens.
3. Americans have the freedoms of speech and religion, they have the right to vote and to a fair trial if accused of a crime, etc.
4. All state and local laws that are in conflict with the Constitution or a federal law are invalid; officials at every level of government are expected to uphold the Constitution.
5. It gives Congress the power to pass laws, the president the power to veto them, and the Supreme Court the power to review them.
6. The document was farseeing and well written. The Founding Fathers intentionally made the amending process difficult.

What Is a Constitution?

A constitution is a plan of government. It describes the kind of government a nation is to have and how that government is to be organized. It also explains the powers of those in control and lists the rights of the citizens they govern. Most countries have constitutions.

The Constitution of the United States is a unique document that has survived for over two hundred years. It is the reason Americans enjoy so many freedoms. In the Preamble, or introduction to the Constitution, the Founding Fathers named the six goals of the document.

Listed below are the six goals the writers of the Constitution included in the Preamble. Describe what you think each one means. Use a dictionary to find the meanings of any words you don't know.

1. To form a more perfect Union _____

_____

_____

2. To establish justice _____

_____

_____

3. To insure domestic tranquility _____

_____

_____

4. To provide for the common defense _____

_____

_____

5. To promote the general welfare _____

_____

_____

6. To secure the blessings of liberty _____

_____

_____

The Need for the Constitution

When America became independent of Great Britain in 1783, the American leaders were reluctant to give the national government too much power. More than 150 years of English rule had convinced them that the best government was the least government.

From 1781 to 1789, the United States functioned under a plan called the Articles of Confederation. (A confederation is a loose group of states with a weak central government.) Each state handled its own affairs and was almost independent. Unfortunately, the lack of a strong national government led to problems. There was confusion and disagreement among the thirteen states. It was difficult to get them to work together. These problems eventually led to the writing of the Constitution of the United States.

Read about the Articles of Confederation in your textbook or in another reference source. Decide if the statements below were true or false under the Articles of Confederation. Write *T* or *F* in each blank.

1. _____ The federal government had the power to tax.

2. _____ Congress could organize a national army.

3. _____ Each state printed its own kind of paper money.

4. _____ The individual states valued their independence.

5. _____ The federal government could make states obey its laws.

6. _____ Congress had the power to manage foreign affairs.

7. _____ Congress could control trade between the states.

8. _____ Congress could make treaties with foreign countries.

9. _____ There was only one house, or division, in Congress.

10. _____ The thirteen states argued about tariffs and boundaries.

11. _____ There was a system of national courts.

The Constitutional Convention

Continuing disagreements over currency (money) and trade under the Articles of Confederation led Virginia to invite all the states to a convention at Annapolis, Maryland, in 1786. Much to the disappointment of James Madison, who had come up with the idea of having the convention, only five states sent delegates to the convention. The states' lack of interest in the convention convinced Madison and others that a much stronger federal government was needed. Alexander Hamilton pointed out that the problems facing the young nation were far too complicated for just five states to consider. He called for a second convention and urged all thirteen states to send representatives.

On May 25, 1787, what became known as the Constitutional Convention assembled in Philadelphia. Every state except Rhode Island sent delegates. In all, there were fifty-five delegates representing twelve states. The convention unanimously elected George Washington as its presiding officer. Besides James Madison and Alexander Hamilton, other distinguished representatives included Edmund Randolph of Virginia, Benjamin Franklin of Pennsylvania, Roger Sherman of Connecticut, and Charles Pinckney of South Carolina.

The group of delegates met to amend (add to and improve) the Articles of Confederation. By the time their work was done, however, they had drafted a new constitution.

Fill each of the following blanks with the correct answer.

1. The Annapolis Convention was the idea of _____.

2. Only _____ states sent delegates to the convention at Annapolis.

3. Poor state attendance at the Annapolis Convention convinced some leaders that

   _____.

4. All of the states sent delegates to the Constitutional Convention in 1787 except

   _____.

5. The Constitutional Convention chose _____ as its presiding officer.

6. Find out more about one of the representatives present at the Constitutional Convention. Write three interesting facts about the man and his life.

   _____

   _____

   _____

   _____

Name_____

James Madison: Father of the Constitution

James Madison of Virginia was one of many great American leaders who helped write the Constitution. He was a small man who weighed only one hundred pounds, but what he lacked in physical size he more than made up for in ability. Largely through his efforts, the system of checks and balances in the United States government came about. This system makes sure that no one branch of the government can dominate the other two. Madison also helped determine the way in which Congress was organized.

Madison wrote most of the final draft of the Constitution as well as the amendments that eventually were called the Bill of Rights. For this reason, he is known in history as the "Father of the Constitution." James Madison later became president of the United States.

Fill in the blanks below to complete the puzzle about James Madison.

1. _____Madison helped write the Constitution.
2. Madison is called the _____ of the Constitution.
3. James Madison was a _____ man.
4. The Constitutional _____ met in Philadelphia.
5. James Madison suggested a system of _____ and balances.
6. Madison was a great _____ leader.
7. Madison wrote the final _____ of the Constitution.
8. Madison weighed one hundred _____.
9. The Bill of _____ is part of the Constitution.
10. James Madison eventually became _____ of the United States.
11. James Madison helped plan the way _____ was set up.
12. _____ was the home state of James Madison.

```
1.              J _ _ _ _
2.            _ A _ _ _ _ _
3.            _ M _ _ _
4.    _ _ _ _ E _ _ _ _ _
5.  _ _ _ _ _ S

6.            _ M _ _ _ _ _ _ _
7.          _ A _ _
8.        _ _ _ _ D _
9.          _ I _ _ _ _
10.    _ _ _ S _ _ _ _ _
11.        _ O _ _ _ _ _ _
12.  _ _ _ _ N _ _
```

Name_____

A Compromise Is Reached

The delegates to the Constitutional Convention were faced with many problems. One of them was determining how the states would be represented in Congress. The large states felt they should have greater representation than the smaller states. The small states believed that all states should have equal power.

Two plans were presented to the convention. One was the Virginia Plan offered by Edmund Randolph. It proposed that a state's number of representatives should be based on population. The second plan was the New Jersey Plan presented by William Paterson. It called for each state to have an equal number of representatives in the legislature.

A compromise was reached through the Connecticut Plan, which was submitted by Roger Sherman. It recommended a two-house legislature consisting of a House of Representatives and a Senate. The number of representatives a state had in the House would be determined by population. Each state would have equal representation in the Senate. This plan was acceptable to most of the delegates.

1. Explain why the Virginia Plan was not a suitable solution to the problem of representation. _____

_____

2. Explain why the New Jersey Plan was not a suitable solution to the problem of representation. _____

_____

3. Explain why the Connecticut Plan was acceptable to most delegates. _____

_____

_____

4. If you were a representative from a small state, would you have accepted the Connecticut Plan as a compromise? Why or why not?_____

_____

_____

5. Describe a time you settled a disagreement with a compromise. _____

_____

_____

Ratifying the Constitution

The Constitution of the United States was signed and adopted on September 17, 1787. Article VII stated that the Constitution would go into effect as soon as nine of the thirteen states ratified, or approved, it. The first state to ratify the Constitution was Delaware on December 7, 1787. The vote at Delaware's ratifying convention was unanimous. The Constitution went into effect on June 21, 1788, when New Hampshire became the ninth state to ratify it. All thirteen states had ratified the Constitution by 1790.

Fill in the information below regarding the ratification votes of various states.

STATE	RATIFICATION VOTE	
	For	Against
Pennsylvania	46	23
Connecticut	128	40
Massachusetts	187	168
New York	30	27
Virginia	89	79
Maryland	63	11

1. In round numbers, _____% of the Connecticut delegates voted for ratification. (Divide the number of votes for ratification by the total number of votes, then multiply by 100 and round.)

2. About _____% of the New York delegates voted for the Constitution.

3. There were _____ delegates at the Massachusetts Convention.

4. The Constitution was ratified in Virginia with a difference of only _____ votes.

5. The state listed with the highest percentage of delegates voting for ratification was _____.

6. In _____, exactly twice as many delegates voted for ratification as for rejection.

7. Which state's votes were nearly even for and against ratification? _____

8. Which state had just over twice as many votes for ratification as New York? _____

9. Which state had the most votes? _____ the fewest? _____

10. How many more of the delegates shown on the chart voted for ratification than against it? _____

The Makeup of Congress

Sections 1, 2, and 3 of Article I of the Constitution address the organization of the legislature. They state that Congress shall be made up of a Senate and a House of Representatives. These sections also list the required qualifications for senators and representatives.

Read the first three sections of Article I, then fill in the information below.

1. A representative in the House must be at least _____ years old.

2. A candidate for the House of Representatives must have been a U.S. citizen for at least _____ years.

3. Representatives are elected for terms of _____ years.

4. A candidate for the Senate must be at least _____ years of age.

5. A senator must have been a citizen of the United States for _____ years.

6. Senators are elected for terms of _____ years.

7. According to Article I, Section 3, senators were chosen by _____. (The Seventeenth Amendment changed this. Senators are now chosen by the voters in their state.)

8. Why do you think the Founding Fathers placed age restrictions on representatives and senators? _____

_____

_____

_____

9. Do you agree with the ages the Founding Fathers chose? Why or why not?

_____

_____

_____

10. Why do you think it's important for representatives and senators to have lived in the United States for a number of years?_____

_____

_____

_____

The Powers of Congress

Article I, Section 8 of the Constitution lists the powers given to Congress. These include the power to do the following:

- collect taxes
- establish post offices
- regulate trade
- make rules for citizenship
- coin money
- set standards for weights and measures
- grant copyrights and patents
- establish federal courts
- declare war
- raise and support an armed force

The powers mentioned above are **expressed powers**. Each is explained in the Constitution. Section 8 of Article I also states that Congress can "make all laws which shall be necessary and proper" to carry out its duties. This is the so-called "elastic clause" that has allowed the federal government to create many national services that the Founding Fathers could not foresee the need for when the Constitution was written. This clause is the basis of Congress's **implied powers**. All powers not expressed in the Constitution are granted to the states and are called **reserved powers**.

Read Article I, Section 8 of the Constitution. On the line next to each of the following phrases, write whether the power falls under the category of expressed, implied, or reserved.

1. to declare war _____

2. to provide for education _____

3. to set standards for television _____

4. to regulate transportation _____

5. to issue marriage licenses _____

6. to determine citizenship rules _____

7. Name another expressed power. _____

8. Name another implied power. _____

9. Name another reserved power. _____

Special Powers of the Senate and the House

Congress is divided into the Senate and the House of Representatives. Each of these two divisions has powers that it alone enjoys. The Senate approves or disapproves treaties with foreign countries as well as all appointments the president makes to the executive and judicial branches of the federal government. It also sits as a jury in impeachment cases brought against federal officials by the House of Representatives. Finally, it chooses the vice president if no candidate receives a majority in the Electoral College.

The Constitution gives the House of Representatives three special powers. First, the House of Representatives initiates all tax bills that go through Congress. Second, only the House of Representatives can bring impeachment charges against federal officials. Third, the House of Representatives selects a president when no candidate receives a majority of the electoral votes.

Remember that the Senate approves appointments to the *federal* government. Must the Senate approve the following government appointments? Write *Yes* or *No* in each blank.

1. _____ a nominee to the U.S. Supreme Court

2. _____ a county judge

3. _____ a nominee for secretary of defense

4. _____ the president's choice for attorney general

5. _____ the head of the Federal Reserve Board

6. _____ the head of a state's highway patrol

Remember that the House of Representatives can try to impeach *federal* officials. Is the House empowered to bring impeachment charges against the following officials? Write *Yes* or *No* in each of the blanks.

7. _____ a federal judge

8. _____ the president

9. _____ a state senator

10. _____ the mayor of Washington, D.C.

11. _____ a state supreme court justice

12. _____ the chief justice of the U.S. Supreme Court

13. _____ a local congressman or congresswoman

14. Do you think the special powers of the Senate or those of the House of Representatives are more important? Explain your answer. _____

_____

_____

Limits to Congress's Power

     Section 9 of Article I is concerned with powers that Congress does not have. For example, except in cases of rebellion or invasion, Congress may not suspend the right of *habeas corpus*. This right guarantees an accused person a speedy appearance before a judge. *Habeas corpus,* which literally means "to produce the body," prevents someone from being arrested or held in jail without just cause.

     Congress also cannot pass a bill of attainder or an *ex post facto* law. A bill of attainder is a law that punishes someone without a trial. An *ex post facto* law makes an act illegal after the act was committed.

     Article I, Section 9 also states that Congress may not tax exports going from one state to another or to another country.

     Use the information above to complete this crossword puzzle.

DOWN

1. *Habeas corpus* means "to produce the _____."
2. The right to a quick appearance before a judge is called the right of _____.
4. What Congress can't do to exports.
5. Congress may not tax goods going between _____ or from a state to another country.

ACROSS

3. A bill of _____ punishes someone without a trial.
6. A law passed to punish someone for an act committed before the act was declared illegal is an _____ law.
7. Article 1, Section 9 of the Constitution limits Congress's _____.

Article I, Section 9 of the Constitution also prevents Congress from giving anyone a title of nobility, such as *king* or *princess*. Why do you think the Founding Fathers forbade this? _____

_____

_____

_____

The Presidency

Article II, Section 1 of the Constitution requires that the president of the United States be at least thirty-five years old. He or she must also be a natural-born citizen who has lived in the United States for at least fourteen years. The president's term in office is set at four years.

The president is actually chosen by the Electoral College. When citizens vote for a president and vice president, they are voting for the group of electors that has pledged to vote for their chosen candidate. Each state has a number of electors equal to its combined number of senators and representatives. A candidate who carries, or wins, a particular state receives all of that state's electoral votes. The candidate with the most electoral votes becomes president. Originally, the person who became vice president was the candidate with the second highest number of electoral votes. This was changed in 1804 by the Twelfth Amendment. Since that time, electors have voted separately for a president and a vice president.

On the lines provided, explain why each of the following people cannot be president of the United States.

1. Boris Strukov, a man who emigrated from the former Soviet Union to the United States in 1975 _____

_____

2. Christine Brown, a 30-year-old state representative from Raleigh, North Carolina

_____

_____

3. Jonathan Blakely, a natural-born U.S. citizen who has lived in France since he was five years old _____

_____

4. What problems might arise from making the runner-up in the presidential election the vice president?_____

_____

_____

_____

_____

The Powers of the President

The powers of the president can be grouped into categories. Diplomatic powers deal with the relations between countries. Military powers relate to the control of the U.S. armed forces. Legislative powers involve law-making. The judicial powers of the president allow him or her to act as a judge. Executive powers involve the carrying out of duties. Sections 2, 3, and 4 of Article II of the Constitution give the president the powers to do the following:

- serve as commander in chief of the armed forces
- make treaties
- appoint ambassadors to foreign countries
- call Congress together for special law-making sessions
- make appointments to the executive branch
- grant pardons and reprieves for federal crimes
- make appointments to the federal courts
- sign and veto bills
- carry out the laws of the United States

Fill in the information below to group the presidential powers listed above.

1. Two of the above powers fall under the category of diplomatic powers. They are

    a._____

    b._____

2. Name the president's military power. _____

3. Two legislative powers of the president are

    a._____

    b._____

4. The president has two judicial powers. They are

    a._____

    b._____

5. List two executive powers of the president.

    a._____

    b._____

6. Most of the president's decisions require the approval of the Senate. Do you think the president's powers should be limited in this way? Why or why not?_____

_____

_____

The Judicial Branch

The federal judicial branch consists of the Supreme Court and the lower courts established by Congress. Federal judges are appointed by the president with the Senate's consent, and they hold office for life. They may be removed only through impeachment.

Article III, Section 1 of the Constitution deals with judicial power in the United States. The Supreme Court was the only court established by the Constitution. The Founding Fathers gave Congress the power to create lower courts as it saw fit. The first district courts were set up in 1789. Today there are about ninety-five district courts. There are also twelve U.S. courts of appeals and a number of lesser courts.

Write the letter of the correct answer in each of the following blanks.

1. _____ Federal judges hold office for
   a. 5 years   **b.** 6 years
   c. life

2. _____ Federal judges are
   a. elected by the voters   **b.** appointed by the president
   c. chosen by the U.S. Senate

3. _____ Which of the following courts did the Constitution establish?
   a. the Supreme Court   **b.** the U.S. district courts
   c. the courts of appeals

4. _____ Federal judges may only be removed from office
   a. by the president   **b.** through the process of impeachment
   c. by a vote of Congress

5. Describe an advantage of having federal judges appointed rather than elected.

   _____

   _____

   _____

   _____

6. Explain an argument in favor of electing federal judges.

   _____

   _____

   _____

   _____

The Jurisdiction of the Federal Courts

The federal courts obtain their authority from the Constitution and federal laws. Some federal courts have only **original jurisdiction**. A court that has original jurisdiction hears cases that have not yet been heard by other courts. Some courts have only **appellate jurisdiction**. They consider and rule on decisions made by lower courts. They do not try cases.

The United States Supreme Court has both original and appellate jurisdiction. It has original jurisdiction in two kinds of cases: those involving ambassadors and other foreign service officials, and those in which a state is a party. It has appellate jurisdiction with regard to cases coming from lower courts.

Most cases involving federal law start in the district courts. There are roughly ninety-five district courts in the U.S. and its possessions. District courts are the only federal courts that use juries. They hear most cases concerned with the violation of a federal law or with disputes between citizens of different states.

U.S. courts of appeals have no original jurisdiction. They only hear cases brought to them for review from the district courts.

Decide if the statements below are true or false. Write *T* or *F* in each blank.

1. _____ The Supreme Court has only appellate jurisdiction.

2. _____ If Butch Johnson is arrested for counterfeiting (a federal offense), his case would be tried in a local court.

3. _____ U.S. district courts are the only federal courts to use juries.

4. _____ U.S. courts of appeals have no original jurisdiction.

5. _____ Cases involving ambassadors are tried in U.S. district courts.

6. _____ Each state has at least one U.S. district court.

7. _____ A defendant who is not satisfied with the decision of a district court can ask a court of appeals to review his or her case.

8. _____ Appellate courts do not try cases.

9. _____ All cases involving federal laws are tried in the Supreme Court.

10. _____ All federal courts have appellate jurisdiction of some kind.

14

The States: Their Relationships with One Another and with the Federal Government

Article IV of the Constitution consists of four sections that deal with the states. Section 1 requires that states accept the legal actions and records of other states. Section 2 provides for the return of a criminal suspect from one state to another upon the request of the governor of the state where a crime was committed. Section 3 gives Congress the power to admit new states and to govern federal territories. Section 4 guarantees that every state will have a republican form of government. It also gives the federal government the responsibility of protecting states from invasion and internal disturbances. (A state governor, for example, can ask the federal government to intervene to help stop a riot.)

Based on the information above, answer the following questions.

1. John and Mary Benson were married in Virginia but one week later moved to Oregon. Is the state of Oregon obligated to recognize their marriage? Why or why not?

_____

_____

_____

2. Extradition refers to a state or country handing an accused criminal over to another state or country. In addition to state extradition agreements, the United States government has extradition treaties with many foreign countries. What do you think would happen if extradition laws did not exist?

_____

_____

_____

3. Section 4 of Article IV of the Constitution guarantees a republican form of government for each state. In your own words, describe a republican form of government. _____

_____

_____

_____

4. Section 2, Part 3 of Article IV no longer has any force in the United States. Read this part of the Constitution and explain why. _____

_____

_____

How Amendments Are Made

The Constitution has been amended, or changed, twenty-seven times. The first ten of these amendments, those known as the Bill of Rights, came into being in 1791. This means that our Constitution has been amended only sixteen times since then! The Founding Fathers wrote a plan of government so workable and farseeing that it has required only a handful of changes in more than two hundred years.

Article V of the Constitution outlines the two ways the document can be amended. First, Congress can propose an amendment by a two-thirds vote of both houses. Second, two-thirds of the states can request that Congress call a special convention to consider a suggested amendment. This second method has never been used.

Once an amendment passes through Congress or a convention, it must be ratified (approved) by three-fourths of the states. There is usually a time limit of seven years for ratification. Congress may, however, extend the time limit if it so desires. It did so with the Equal Rights Amendment, which has thus far failed to be ratified.

Fill in the correct numbers in the following four sentences.

1. To become part of the Constitution, an amendment must be ratified by at least _____ states.

2. There are one hundred U.S. senators. Two-thirds of them must vote in favor of a proposed amendment. This means that at least _____ senators must support it.

3. Two-thirds of the states can petition Congress to call a special convention to propose an amendment. Therefore, at least _____ states must be in favor of such a convention.

4. The Twenty-Seventh Amendment was first proposed in 1789. It was ratified in 1992. How many years did it take for the amendment to be ratified? _____

5. Why do you think the Founding Fathers made the amending process difficult?

_____

_____

6. Choose one amendment from the Bill of Rights and explain why it was an important addition to the Constitution. _____

_____

_____

_____

_____

The Supremacy of the Federal Government

Article VI of the Constitution requires that judges in every state recognize the Constitution as the supreme law of the land. The same holds true for all laws made by Congress. If a judge finds that a state law is in conflict with the Constitution, he or she must rule in favor of the Constitution.

Article VI also states that all federal and state officials are bound to uphold the Constitution. It concludes by affirming that no government employee shall ever be subjected to a religious test as a condition of employment.

1. Could a state pass a law that allows children to vote in presidential elections? Why or why not? _____

_____

_____

_____

2. In the early days of our country, Chief Justice John Marshall established the Supreme Court's power of judicial review. This means that the Supreme Court can overturn any federal or state law that is in violation of the Constitution. On the lines below, invent three state laws that would surely be overturned by the Supreme Court. Explain why each would be unconstitutional.

   a. _____

   _____

   _____

   _____

   b. _____

   _____

   _____

   _____

   c. _____

   _____

   _____

   _____

3. What part of Article VI supports the idea of the separation of church and state? Explain. _____

_____

_____

The Bill of Rights

The writers of the Constitution did not think it was necessary to list the individual rights of the people when they wrote the document in 1787. Several states, however, refused to ratify the new plan of government until a Bill of Rights was added. This was done in 1791, and the first ten amendments became a part of the Constitution.

The First Amendment guarantees the freedoms of religion, speech and the press, assembly, and petition. People may practice the religion of their choice. They may say or print whatever they wish, as long as it is true. People may meet peacefully and discuss issues without fear of reprisal (the use of force). Finally, they can petition or complain to the government about things they do not like.

Each freedom listed in the First Amendment, however, has limitations. Although people are allowed to express their opinions, for example, they are not allowed to say or print things that would harm someone's reputation. Obscenities are not permitted in public. Any speech that endangers lives or property is also prohibited.

To the left of each of the statements below, write *Yes* if it is something a citizen is permitted to do or *No* if it is an act that is not allowed.

1. _____ Give a speech before a large gathering of people and express opinions about the president's abilities.

2. _____ Write a letter to the White House threatening to harm the president.

3. _____ Yell "fire" in a movie theater when there is no fire.

4. _____ Write a letter for the editorial page of a newspaper in which you criticize a state legislator.

5. _____ Make up a story about a teacher that causes him or her to be reprimanded or even fired.

6. _____ Participate in a street demonstration that causes traffic problems.

7. _____ Circulate a petition calling for the repeal of an unpopular law.

8. _____ Give an opinion on an issue being discussed at a local school board meeting.

9. _____ Use profanity in public.

10. _____ Require employees to attend religious services.

The Right to Bear Arms

    The Second Amendment safeguards the right of citizens to keep or bear arms. When it was adopted in 1791, this amendment referred to the right of states to maintain a militia for their own security. In recent years, the right to bear arms has erupted into a controversy that has sometimes divided the nation. On one hand, there are those who support some kind of gun control in the hope of reducing violence. On the other hand, opponents of gun control say that people have a Constitutional right to own any guns they choose.

    The Third Amendment guarantees the security of the home. Soldiers may not be stationed in any house unless the owner agrees. Congress could, however, pass a law during wartime that would allow for this if it were necessary. This amendment was added because Americans thought it was unfair that the government in Britain forced people to house British soldiers.

    The Fourth Amendment protects one's home and property against unreasonable searches and seizures. Under most circumstances, police officers must obtain a warrant from a judge in order to search someone's house or other possessions.

1. On the lines below, describe one argument for and one argument against gun control. _____

_____

_____

_____

What is your opinion on the issue? _____

_____

_____

2. Do you think it is fair to force people to open their homes to soldiers during wartime? Why or why not? _____

_____

_____

_____

3. Describe a situation in which the police might be able to obtain a warrant to search a house or a building. _____

_____

_____

_____

_____

The Rights of the Accused

The Fifth through Eighth amendments outline the following rights for people accused of criminal acts.

- They cannot be tried twice for the same crime.
- They cannot be forced to testify against themselves.
- They are entitled to due process of law.
- They have the right to a speedy trial before a jury of their peers, or equals.
- They must be told of the charges against them.
- They have the right to a lawyer and to witnesses in their defense.
- They cannot be subjected to excessive bail or fines, nor to any cruel or unusual punishment.
- Only a grand jury can indict (charge) someone with a capital crime (a crime punishable by death).

In addition, the Constitution states that people cannot have their private property taken away without receiving fair payment from the government.

Match the following terms with their definitions.

1. ____ To charge with an offense or crime

2. ____ Kind of crime that is punishable by death

3. ____ Group that decides whether there is enough evidence to bring an accused to trial

4. ____ Person who saw something happen

5. ____ Too much; too great

6. ____ Answer questions under oath in a court of law

7. ____ Money paid to release an accused person from jail until a trial is held

8. ____ One's equal

9. ____ A guarantee that someone's life, liberty, or property cannot be taken away unfairly

a. witness

b. indict

c. testify

d. grand jury

e. due process

f. capital

g. excessive

h. bail

i. peer

10. Do you believe that people accused of crimes deserve all of these rights? Why or why not?_____

_____

_____

Rights Reserved for the People
and the States

The Ninth Amendment assures the people of the states that they have rights other than those listed in the first eight amendments.

The Tenth Amendment explains that the states have all the powers that are not specifically given to the federal government. These powers include the powers to hold elections and to establish school systems. The states have authority over marriages and divorces. States also have what are called "policing powers." This means that a state is responsible for the safety and well-being of its people. It can require vaccinations for school children and licenses for such professionals as doctors, teachers, and lawyers. It can issue licenses to those who hunt, fish, and drive motor vehicles. It can also set speed limits on state highways. In addition, restaurants must follow specific health rules determined by the state. Finally, the citizens of a state can look to the state police to safeguard their homes and highways.

States share some powers with the federal government. These are called concurrent powers. They include the powers to tax, to pass laws, and to punish criminals.

1. List five policing powers that states have.

    _____

    _____

    _____

2. List three powers states share with the federal government.

    _____

    _____

    _____

3. Write *S* or *F* before each statement to indicate whether it is a state's responsibility or the responsibility of the federal government.
    a. _____ Issue a teaching license to someone who has applied and has met all the requirements
    b. _____ Make a treaty with a foreign country
    c. _____ Set health codes for restaurants
    d. _____ Issue a marriage license
    e. _____ Declare war

Jurisdiction of the Federal Courts; Election of the President and Vice President

The Eleventh Amendment, ratified in 1794, states that a federal court cannot hear a case brought against a state by a citizen of another state or country. This amendment took away a power given to the federal government under Article III of the Constitution.

Article II, Section 1 of the Constitution states that the candidate with the second highest number of votes in the presidential election becomes vice president. The Twelfth Amendment changed the way the Electoral College votes for president and vice president. The electors now vote separately for the two offices. If no candidate receives a majority of the votes for president, the election is decided in the House of Representatives. The Senate follows a similar procedure in electing the vice president when no candidate has attained a majority.

There are 538 votes in the Electoral College. Use this information and the figures below to solve the following problems.

State	Electoral Votes
California	44
Wyoming	3
Illinois	22
Florida	25
Missouri	11
Maine	9

1. What percentage of the total electoral vote does California have? (Divide the number of California votes by the total number of votes, then multiply by 100.) _____%

2. Missouri has _____% of the total electoral vote.

3. What is the least number of electoral votes a candidate needs to become president? _____

4. What percentage of the total electoral vote do California and Florida have when combined? _____%

5. Which of the states listed above has the smallest percentage of the electoral vote? _____ What percentage does it have? _____%

6. The total combined votes of the six states above make up _____% of the total electoral vote.

The Civil War Amendments

Three amendments passed between 1865 and 1870, as a result of the Civil War, were aimed at granting ex-slaves and other groups the same rights enjoyed by most Americans. After the Civil War, Abraham Lincoln's Emancipation Proclamation abolished slavery in Confederate states that were still fighting against the Union. The Thirteenth Amendment, however, abolished slavery in *all* of the United States and in any place subject to its jurisdiction. The Fourteenth Amendment granted citizenship to all people born in the United States and to those who are naturalized citizens. This made ex-slaves who were born in the United States citizens.

The Fifteenth Amendment, ratified in 1870, extended the right to vote to all adult male citizens regardless of race or color. For many years after its ratification, however, some states used poll taxes and literacy tests as a way to prevent black Americans from voting. (A poll tax is a fixed amount of money every adult citizen is required to pay. In the past, people were not allowed to vote in national elections if their taxes were not paid.) This practice continued until Congress passed the Voting Rights Act of 1965.

Answer the questions below.

1. How could a poll tax or a literacy test have been used to prevent someone from voting? _____

_____

_____

2. Why are these three amendments sometimes called the Civil War amendments?

_____

_____

3. All adult U.S. citizens now have the right to vote. Many people do not take advantage of this right, however. Do you think it is important for every adult to vote? Explain your answer. _____

_____

_____

_____

4. A naturalized citizen is a person who becomes a citizen of a country in which he or she was not born. When a person becomes a naturalized citizen of the United States, he or she must give up citizenship to any other nation. Do you think you would ever consider becoming a citizen of another country? Why or why not?

_____

_____

_____

The Income Tax and the Direct Election of U.S. Senators

The first income tax was imposed by Congress in 1861. It was a three percent tax on incomes over $800. This tax was increased several times during the Civil War, but it was discontinued in 1870. A second tax of two percent was initiated in 1894 on incomes over $4,000. It was declared unconstitutional just one year later. The Sixteenth Amendment in 1913 gave the federal government the power to tax the wages of all working people. It called for a graduated tax, one that is based on how much a person earns. Those with higher incomes pay a greater portion of their wages in income taxes to the federal government.

Also in 1913, the Seventeenth Amendment became a part of the Constitution. It provided for the direct election of U.S. senators by the voters of the respective states. Until that time, senators were chosen by the state legislatures.

How much income tax would a person earning $40,000 a year pay at the following tax rates? Use the space provided to figure the answers.

1. 16% $_____   2. 13% $_____

3. 11% $_____   4.   8% $_____

5.   3% $_____   6. 14% $_____

7. 10% $_____   8.   9% $_____

9.   4% $_____   10.   6% $_____

11. Do you think it is fair for the government to tax a citizen's income? Why or why not?

_____

_____

_____

_____

12. Those who earn more pay a higher portion of their income to the government. Do you think this is a fair way to tax? Can you think of a fairer way?_____

_____

_____

_____

_____

Prohibition and Its Repeal

A reform movement that swept across America during the end of the 19th century led to the passage of the Eighteenth Amendment in 1919. For years, groups like the Woman's Christian Temperance Union and the Anti-Saloon League had campaigned for laws to ban all forms of alcoholic drinks. Some people believed alcohol led to poverty, illness, and family problems. Others believed saloons supported corrupt political systems. Many states had taken matters into their own hands and passed such legislation in the years before World War I. In 1919, the Eighteenth Amendment was added to the Constitution. It forbade the manufacture, sale, or transportation of alcoholic beverages anywhere in the United States.

This amendment was unpopular with many Americans and was virtually impossible to enforce. Instead of the positive effects on behavior that supporters had hoped for, the Eighteenth Amendment helped to create a crime problem that existed in America until 1933 when the amendment was repealed. The 1920s, often called the Prohibition Era, became the age of moonshine (whiskey made illegally) and gang warfare. Between 1920 and 1930, there were more than five hundred gang-related murders in the United States.

Few complained when the Twenty-First Amendment in 1933 repealed the Eighteenth Amendment and brought the Prohibition Era to an end.

1. What was the original goal of Prohibition? _____

_____

_____

2. The Eighteenth Amendment is the only amendment to be repealed. Why was the prohibition amendment repealed? _____

_____

_____

_____

3. Do you think the Eighteenth Amendment intruded on Americans' personal lives too much? Should the government ever be allowed to control such personal issues? Explain your answers._____

_____

_____

_____

_____

_____

Extended Voting Rights

Between the years 1920 and 1971, four amendments assured the right to vote for Americans who had previously been denied this privilege. In 1920, the Nineteenth Amendment granted women the right to vote. Some states, Wyoming being the first, had allowed women to vote as early as 1869.

The Twenty-Third Amendment, ratified in 1961, gave the citizens of Washington, D.C. the right to vote for president and vice president for the first time. Until then, the residents were not permitted to vote in presidential elections because the District of Columbia is not part of any state.

The Twenty-Fourth Amendment, ratified in 1964, outlawed poll taxes. This amendment, along with the Voting Rights Act of 1965, ended voting discrimination.

The Twenty-Sixth Amendment of 1971 lowered the voting age in America to eighteen. Several states had done this previously on their own. There was strong sentiment in America that if citizens over eighteen were old enough to fight and die for their country, they were old enough to vote.

Place the following events in chronological order by writing the numbers 1 to 6 on the lines.

1. _____ The Twenty-Fourth Amendment is ratified.

2. _____ Women in Wyoming receive the right to vote.

3. _____ Women nationwide are granted the right to vote.

4. _____ The nationwide voting age is lowered to eighteen.

5. _____ Residents of the District of Columbia are permitted to vote in presidential elections.

6. _____ Congress passes the Voting Rights Act.

7. Do you think the voting age should be even lower than 18? Support your opinion with at least two reasons.

_____

_____

_____

_____

_____

_____

Changes Regarding Congress and the Presidency

The Twentieth, Twenty-Second, and Twenty-Fifth Amendments eliminated problems that had arisen earlier concerning both Congress and the presidency. Recall that presidential and Congressional elections are held in November. Until 1933, the newly-elected president did not take office until March 4. This meant that there was a period of four months following the election when the White House was occupied by a "lame duck," or outgoing, president. Little was usually accomplished during these months. The same held true for a newly-elected Congress that did not take office for many months after the elections. The Twentieth Amendment solved these problems. After 1933, the incoming president took office on January 20 and the new Congress convened on January 3.

Amendment Twenty-Two of 1951 limited the president and vice president to two consecutive terms. Prior to this amendment, Franklin Delano Roosevelt was elected four times and would have served sixteen years had he not died in 1945.

The Twenty-Fifth Amendment, ratified in 1967, addressed the problem of presidential disability and succession. It states that the vice president shall become acting president should the president become disabled or for some other reason not be able to carry out his or her duties. It also provides for the president to choose a vice president (with the approval of Congress) should that office become vacant.

The final amendment, the Twenty-Seventh, states that Congress cannot pass immediate pay raises for itself. It was ratified in 1992.

Write *T* for true or *F* for false next to each of the following statements.

1. ____ Franklin Delano Roosevelt served sixteen years as president.

2. ____ A president is now limited to two consecutive terms.

3. ____ Until 1933, a newly-elected president did not take office until March 4 following the election.

4. ____ The House of Representatives selects a vice president if that office becomes vacant.

5. ____ A new Congress convenes in the month of December.

6. ____ The Speaker of the House of Representatives becomes acting president if the president is disabled.

7. ____ A "lame duck" president is one who is re-elected to a second term.

8. ____ Presidential elections are held in November.

9. ____ The vice president selects a president if the president becomes disabled.

10. ____ Congress cannot pass an immediate pay raise for itself.

Checking Your Understanding
of the Constitution

1. Why is it important for a nation to have a constitution? _____
_____
_____
_____

2. What kinds of information are included in a constitution? _____
_____
_____
_____

3. Identify some of the fundamental rights and freedoms guaranteed by the United States Constitution. _____
_____
_____
_____
_____

4. Why is the Constitution considered to be the supreme law of the land? _____
_____
_____
_____
_____

5. In what ways does the Constitution provide for a system of checks and balances in law-making? _____
_____
_____
_____
_____

6. Why do you think the U.S. Constitution has been amended only twenty-seven times? _____
_____
_____
_____